IN SOMEONE ELSE'S HOUSE

POEMS

Christian Barter writes about love and mortality and justice and, over and over, the difficult and amazing fact of our separateness from everyone else—not the Capital Letter versions of those feelings, but the ones that sweep through you listening to music, or musing late at night, or just driving along. Barter won't waste your time with archness, or meta-meta twiddling, or disposable Cool. He's a warmly funny and passionately thoughtful poet whose characteristic note is a hurt yet irrepressible joy. His lean and expert poems are the real thing: they have something to say, they are moving, they matter.

—James Richardson

There are poets who can bring us to tears; there are poets who can make us ponder vast societal and existential issues; there are poets whose irony moves us at once to ruefulness and to dark laughter; there are poets who fruitfully challenge our intellectual capacities. But Christian Barter is that rarest of writers, the one who can make us react in all these ways, and often simultaneously. Such multiplicity of response, he teaches us, is our sole way of dealing with the strange sense that, at least metaphorically, we are always in someone else's house. Barter everywhere considers what I must call—though the label is vexingly reductive — the nature of human truth. This book is a marvel.

—Sydney Lea

IN SOMEONE ELSE'S HOUSE

POEMS

Christian Barter

BkMk BkMk Press
University of Missouri-Kansas City

BkMk Press
University of Missouri-Kansas City
5101 Rockhill Road
Kansas City, Missouri 64110
(816) 235-2558 (voice)
(816) 235-2611 (fax)
www.umkc.edu/bkmk

Financial assistance for this project has been provided by
the Missouri Arts Council, a state agency.

Cover Art: Dan MIller
Author Photo: Ann Arbor
Book design: Susan L. Schurman
Managing Editor: Ben Furnish
Associate Editor: Michelle Boisseau

BkMk Press wishes to thank Linda D. Brennaman Kara McKeever,
Andrew Johnson, Samantha Morris, Gregory Van Winkle.
Printer: McNaughton & Gunn, Inc.

Library of Congress Cataloging-in-Publication Data

Barter, Christian, 1969-
[Poems. Selections]
In someone else's house : poems / Christian Barter.
pages cm
Summary: "These poems reflect on such varied themes as friendship, love, mortality, war and the Middle East, the environment, and life as a single man in the early 21st century United States with references to classical as well as popular culture and recent nostalgia"--Provided by publisher.
ISBN 978-1-886157-85-9 (pbk. : alk. paper)
I. Title.
PS3602.A8386I57 2012
811'.6--dc23
2012037229

This book is set in Cheltenham ITC Pro and Baker Signet.

Acknowledgments

I thank the following magazines for originally publishing the following poems:

The Agriculture Reader:	John and Jackie Kennedy on a Boat Deck, 1960
The Cimarron Review:	When I Found Out I Was Dying
Hotel Amerika:	Alien
	Sonnets to Elise
The Literary Review:	The Phoenix
	Providence
New York Quarterly:	Things I've Forgotten
Pleiades	Kicking Russell Out of the Band
Ploughshares:	Heisenberg
	To the Unborn
Poet Lore:	Marcelle
	Where Sullivan Met Franklin
Post Road:	People in History

"The Phoenix" is featured on the website *Poems from the Fishouse* and in the print anthology *From the Fishouse: An Anthology of Poems that Sing, Rhyme, Resound, Syncopate, Alliterate and Just Plain Sound Great* (Persea Books). "Providence" appeared on *Verse Daily.*

And thanks to my friends who helped me figure out what I was doing with these poems: Jeffrey Thomson, James Richardson, Michael Morse, and Alex Halberstadt.

IN
SOMEONE ELSE'S HOUSE
POEMS

1

2

3

Things I've Forgotten

All my best first lines for instance
that come to me while I'm driving so fast
my self lags behind or when I'm riding
the elevator up into sleep and the unseen streets
are dropping away below me how exactly
Socrates proved all knowledge
is remembered the names
of women I slept with who
assassinated whom the books
I read last year the faces of some how it felt
to be eighteen nineteen twenty-
seven or yesterday morning with Sonny Rollins
blowing the doors from some passageway reeking
of 1965 and a thirst I was born with how
to get anywhere I've only been once
and some places I've been going all my life blowing
like hope and death had woken up in the same bed
and were trying to disentangle themselves it had
something to do with a boy and the spaces
inside of squares what happened
between the fall of Rome and the Battle
of Hastings when exactly
Christianity gave up on poverty when
Mesopotamia fell when Crete when
Greece when Rome when Byzantium the Saxons
the Mayans the Franks the Visigoths
the eunuchs the mammoths
the dodo birds at least one of them was
The Idiot where salvation is no better
than a seizure or is that what he meant who said
we have seen the enemy what it was
I thought I needed to say with sleep
pulling up on my shores like

stout Cortés who Proserpine was what
Sisyphus did when it
was I last knew and the time
before that what was said between
so many of us before the long stutters
of our fuckings and sleep taking over
like a stunned vice president

At the Sleep Clinic

On the TV, Sandra Bullock, an upstart lawyer
from humble beginnings, is impressing the hell
out of Hugh Grant, an innocently withering,
billionaire playboy, in any number of legal ways
as Keith, a well-meaning and competent
sleep-study technologist, attaches electrodes
to my head and chest—my well-meaning,
but possibly also upstart, head and chest.
You can tell right away they are going to
hit it off—he's screwing everything in Gucci,
she's staying long hours doing his legal work
in unflattering clothes and what people in Hollywood
must think is bad hair, dropping things
and conversing adorably stiffly as Keith has me
lean forward to get a band around my chest
and I joke, "I'd better not try to escape,"
a tangle of wires hanging off me like some
chieftain. Billionaire playboy
is chatting up some chick in a bar
but is also on the phone to the upstart lawyer,
still at the office, of course, who gets
the chick on the phone and sneaks in something
about a rash on Hugh Grant's crotch—which we know
all too well means she wants him herself,
but damned if either one of them
is onto it yet. "So we can tell
what stage of sleep you're in," Keith explains
about the electrodes on my head. Someone
is gliding through an endless wilderness
with a glittering SUV. By the time
I am slid into bed with my heartbeats and brainwaves
ready to go public, there has been some kind
of hurtful crisis and Hugh is preparing

to demolish a community center and Sandra
is bitterly disappointed that fortunes
are amassed in this way but worse, finds him
half-clothed with her half-clothed replacement
in some ritzy suite. "Make a snoring sound,"
Keith tells me through a speaker,
then count to five and twitch my toes,
and all kinds of other horseshit so I miss
exactly how the transformation takes place—
as I always miss exactly how
the transformation takes place—but Hugh is making
a speech to Sandra: he has sacrificed
a certain small portion of his billions in order
to rectify the situation with the community center—
and she kicks him out, but this can't be it. "Just try
to sleep normally," Keith is telling me.
And sure enough, there they are together
on a sidewalk, billionaire playboy
and idealistic upstart—rich as Trump
and principled as Harriet Tubman—
kissing as though he were heading off
to the Great War. And I shut off the light
and lie there wondering if I'll sleep,
until I do.

The Future

Do I just want to be young again? It's such
a petty wish, at forty, watching
Riggins and Lyla kissing on TV. She is
all right after all that he's come knocking
at her forbidden door with his
hard-drinking, tough-guy ways and he
has listed the reasons she must be, especially
that he has made the football team and says,
"There's just no one I want to celebrate with
other than you," outside her bungalow
in a Texas late-afternoon, a warm
and auburn place against the wall, a place
I suddenly feel I'll get to myself
eventually. Recently I found
a book of photos of RISD students
taken forty years ago and I have
not been able to shake the feeling
that those spare, paint-flecked apartments
with their floors worn smooth,
those soap-box-square cars, bright as teeth,
those eye-shadowed faces over-
come and feigning boredom, are somehow
still a part of the future. And when I dream
of ex-lovers they are always
coming up the stairs or walking towards me
on a yellow trail, we haven't yet
made love or moved to the town
that will end our streak—the heart of things
is yet to come. I don't know where else
to put all this happiness, I guess.
I don't know what other door to knock on
this tired, this elated.
I wouldn't even *want* there to be one.

Stars

Down the driveway, standing on the Russell Farm Road,
nothing but stars over my neighbor's field
and over my neighbor's house which crouches
under them with its lit windows,
cozy and distant as a research station.
Between the bare branches left hanging
like threads on cut shirt sleeves, stars tingle,
whole galaxies for the leaves that now fill ditches.
And down the road toward the impoundment lot
stars fill the river that cuts the trees' black banks.

I stand in my work coat, dizzy with nicotine,
straining my head back like a boy drinking rain
to see more of them, star behind star,
rich milk of stars, ripe fruit of stars,
cast jewels, lit snowflakes, cityscapes of stars
through every window the night has thrown open,
through every perforation in the woods,
and step on the cigarette I've dropped in the road,
nothing but stars, stars falling away forever
beneath the veneer of dark that supports my feet.

Marcelle

She came to my dorm room and stayed the night with me
a couple times—rare bouts of innocence
in those days of always shoving in like a pushy fan
trying to get to the stage—

and kept her clothes on, sleeping in jeans
like we were trapped in an airport or something,
snuggling up to me with that nonplussed look of hers
and letting me kiss her, I think,

for whatever that would have been worth.
It was absolutely nothing that brought us together—
perhaps a class, or that she lived three doors down
and left her door open while she typed,

her studious, generous face like a lamp left on
in some old, empty house, me coasting
on marbles home with a cigarette going—me,
who got in the habit of stopping to talk maybe

just because my ears were ringing
with the silence of the place—and yet
it is her I am thinking of tonight with a tenderness
that is almost like sleep it is so natural

and so safe from the sweaty effort
of another day walking in my heavy armor.
It's a nation-founding myth that years
bring wisdom. I still have no idea

why she slid into bed beside me
those two nights, weeks apart, saying
nothing, perhaps, as would have been her way
at such a time, clasping me in her sweatered arms

as though sex were a thing of the past
and new snow building on the runway.

Where Sullivan Met Franklin

I hate being back there, where Sullivan met Franklin,
where the school bus I was on went one more stop
past Phil's house, then turned around cussingly
where the road went dirt—but yesterday, again,
I have been asked if you are my father and this morning
I am thinking of passing your self-built house, and not
in the usual vein of nothingness I have for you
who were not there since I turned four, but wondering
how it was for you, for any man, to see that indifferent
school bus pass and double back whereon
his son was on one side or the other. I wonder,
ex-father, did you come to the window looking
for my fat face, or hide in the back where the kitchen was
in case I was looking for you? Or pay no tithing
to those overlords of Should and Shame and How It Was
and How It Must Still Be? I hope, Philip Barter,
you paid them nothing—whatever was left of the nothing
you paid my mother. But when has hope had anything
to do with life? School, with its sunlit lawns
forever trapped outside, where Sean and Tom
would brush by me in the halls with the same brush, always
came toward us until we got there. Fuck all that.
There was nothing to be done about it then
and there's certainly nothing now, from my little house
on a dead-end road, where the bus goes by each way
each morning, each way each afternoon.
Or have I spent all my nothing on you?

The Final Movement of a Late Quartet

on Beethoven's Opus 131 in C-sharp minor

Until the last three hammer strokes batter
through its dense walls with the light of C-sharp major, this

is the darkest music we know and yet
there is no struggle here, no pain,

just death strolling around in some city it made
within us long ago, death's version of joy,

and even the lilting, major-key second theme
is not some hope flowering over the grave or even

a long last look from our sweetest love,
but rather, death smelling the air in some

garden it planted within us long ago.
Until the last three hammer strokes

batter through with the life of C-sharp major,
no wonder we're inclined to think

these places are not that important to us—though strange,
and undeniably beautiful—we who sit

with our iPods in the thicknesses
of late-March sun, our lovers creaking the floor downstairs,

deep in the citadel of our years.

Things I Would Have Said about Me When I'm Gone

That he loved, when he could, everything that he could
That he resolved that little problem he had of being hated
Nothing
That he kept a massive list on the wall, and all the important things
had checkmarks by them
That he resolved that little problem he had of hating everyone else
That in spite of certain shortcomings
That because of an unquenchable thirst
That it turned out he was right about the thyroid problem
That who cares what we say about him now
Certainly not him
That now all those mistakes appear more as the calculated moves
of a superior being
That he did his worst, and we withstood it
Nothing. Please
That we're sorry about slapping the back of his head on the school bus
That *dead* is probably not the right choice of words
That what is life for, if not to drink coffee and stare at the chiseled,
shining trees
in the long, continuous morning of our unemployment
That yet, for all this, few would call him self-centered
Not now, certainly
That his greatest fear was of living forever
That for those of you in the nosebleed seats
That several witnesses have sworn he was behind this rock
That we're sorry about the rejection slips, and the bad coffee in Idaho,
and the time we wouldn't make love to him when he followed us down
Myrtle Street
That few would call him a total, screaming asshole
A toxin to those to whom he was closest
Not now, certainly
Did I mention the checkmarks?
That after that, the brain can be thawed back out
That due to an unfillable hole
An unseeable light
That given what's happened, I can't explain this joy

Alien

In *Alien*, when Sigourney Weaver
has stripped down to her panties and shrink-wrap T
in order to sleep for ten months
in a pod that will keep her alive all the way
to earth but has spied the alien
drooling in the machinery and motherboards,
having somehow crept onto the shuttlecraft
she is trying to escape it with and she's
backed against that futuristic wall
with those low, interior space lights shining
on her smooth legs and torso and moving
in the slow-mo of trying not to wake
someone tangled in sheets with you so that
the camera shooting from somewhere around
her knees catches every sweet glimmer
of her ripe and athletic body, who

can blame us for forgetting that this is
outer space where the only oxygen
for a million miles is in that tender
spacecraft, or that a hideous, giant,
insect-like creature with crooked
dinosaur teeth and snot for saliva
may not only plant its disgusting eggs
in her living body, but slither off
at earth and do the same to all
of humanity? Who can expect us

to remember our own lovers upstairs
lying on their sides reading
real literature, where sexy and tough
won't buy you a nanosecond, lying there
aging away with life-sustaining

fat clinging like the Spock grip
to various parts of them, our lovers
who took the call every time we had
the inexplicable weakness and took us
back even after the shouting episode
behind the lady at Shaw's with all
the coupons—who,

when Sigourney is stretching that one leg
so slowly sideways to get in
to the protective suit and the greenish light
is x-raying through the fabric
of her tiny T—who, when even
of the alien there is only to remind us
a low, carnivorous, off-screen
growl—and of earth's
tenuous fate, just the fact of her breathing?

Visiting

We are visiting, on Christmas Day, the Orrs,
our family friends since their Chrissie and I
were tiny. Now she is large
and lives upstairs at forty but is
disconcertingly exactly the same
and her mother is still baking
Christmas stars, still smiles the same
though osteoporosis is curling her
like a too-thin toast. And Mr. Orr,
firm-handed shop teacher the lobstermen
and roofers around here still call
Mr. Orr, now can't remember
anything except his stories, which have
found each other in the dark and blended
seamlessly as some surrealist's
workday: the car that broke in half
pulling into the school, a cannon buried
upside-down in a field somewhere,
men loading crates of ice
into backs of trucks. "I think I've left
my pickup running," he says, then
sits back down. And wasn't it just
yesterday, isn't it still
now that Chrissie and I and my sister
are chasing each other on the steep front lawn
in a 1970s summer,
the porch lights mapping vast
islands of shadow, the grownups
safe in the bright house, drinking
wine and coffee and laughing all
at once among the mumbling as though
the night kept peeking out behind its
frightening costume? As now

as this is: Cathy at the door, asking,
“Next year, right?” like
a guess and Mr. Orr’s pickup
idling in the drivveway

Convalescence

You sitting on a bench in Philly in the heat,
your laugh, even through the phone, the single ripple
that makes the vast lake's surface visible,
which is something, today, I can appreciate,
my blood sugar righted, rested, drinking coffee,
a bird amped in a treetop, single lines
of Larkin and Lowell tracing whole designs.
All loves spring from the same soil, don't they.
How to remain there is the only question,
my body sprouting inside itself, one thought
becoming the next by music or dream. "Oh, perfect,"
you said when you answered, just sat down
in front of your sister's on that car-jammed street
where one huge elm has dived up through the concrete.

To the Unborn

We have smoked all the cigarettes
and sold the last pack years ago
but I think you'll thank us once you read
the research—that much
we took upon ourselves. So,
remember: smoking kills. Beware
of radiation, mercury and ground-level ozone,
and for God's sakes, wear your seatbelts
in whatever kind of wacky cars you make.
We've left some ideas for those,
by the way. What else? Enjoy
the place—we wish it could have been
better, but we had long
retirements, most of us, and you know
how expensive *that* can be. How time
flies! I must admit, we were
caught off guard by some things. We hope
you get along, but if you don't,
there are plenty of nuclear weapons
for you to use—just keep in mind,
they really should be launched by
democratic nations, otherwise
all hell could break loose. Sorry
about the farmland, but at least there's a copy
of the latest food pyramid lying around
somewhere. So eat healthy!
And remember to take life one day at a time.
Lord knows it gets by quickly. The secret
of our happiness, I'd say,
was in accepting what we could not change.

Heisenberg

We interfere with what we know by knowing it.
We interfere with what we do by doing it.
We interfere with what we love by loving it.

I guess you could say we're the causes of our own loneliness.

We interfere with what we watch by watching it.
We interfere with what we write by writing it.
We interfere with what we think by thinking it.
We interfere with where we go by going there.

We are like Midas, or Medusa.

We interfere with life by living it.

In fact, one definition of perfection is simply
the way things are when we are not around.
Or might have been if I hadn't said so.

One question, though: is all this actually true?
We interfere with what we ask by asking it.

If there is a God we will
surely ruin him by believing in him.

And yet we must exist, correct?

Don't answer that! You
who remain you only by your absence.

Cassandra

"The pain! The terror!..." Agamemnon, *Aeschylus*

1

In retrospect, it's clear as prophesy:
of course they'd blame their deafness to revelation
on anyone but themselves—their Olympian scapegoats
would serve as well as ever: "Apollo's curse."
The only priapic "god" to force himself
on *me* had the hydra head and hydra-stink
of one blue-balled Greek lackey after another,
and the only curse about hearing the truth
was the same old curse the truth was born with:
most men would sooner die than believe it.
And die they do, as eagerly as a rape-train.
Surprised to hear me talk like this? Did you expect:
"The pain, the terror! The birth pang of the seer
who tells the truth—it whirls, me, oh"? [1]
Ever knew anyone who told the truth
and sounded like that? If they could make me seem
hysterical they'd look a lot less stupid,
so that's the kind of press I've gotten: hot,
and right—but so what? She was *weird.*

2

I *was* weird, I guess. I kept to myself, mainly.
I wasn't very into boys, or religion.
The dreams kept me busy from a young age.
They were so much more real than what was supposed to be real:
the normal things of life—the gossip, sports,
small talk, the endless speeches of Hector
and Paris and my poor old father, who thought
that they were the only virtue left on earth
the way they went on about the infidels
gathering outside as though they hadn't brought
that shit upon themselves. The dreams were so

beautiful in a way life couldn't be:
the pure brilliance of the sky, the clear pools,
the sheer cliffs towering at the edge of things.
If there *are* gods they see things no more purely.
They were, of course, the things of life, and yet
as different from life as you can imagine.
Oh, the beautiful horse I saw! It stood
at dawn on a silent, sleeping field, the soldiers
gone from the shores, the eye-blue ocean reaching
beyond the horizon, the silence of the fields
like a place in itself, the horse so tall and serious
and forlorn, this inexplicable great toy,
this orphan, this symbol, this strange guest of peace
which seemed to *want* peace, down to its wheeled feet.

3

And then the choking heat, the knife of panic—
through punctures, the bodies disgorging themselves in the streets
which stank with blood, my father vomiting blood
from his sad old mouth onto his young man's armor
like a child ruining the one toy he loves,
the smoke like a sopping blanket in my lungs,
the half-toothed stinking Greeks with their unsheathed pricks—
It took waking to make sense of it: that death
would come as this strange gift on a perfect day
when we'd won the battle we'd thought was for our lives
and the air smelled of ocean, wheat and flowers. Death
would enter as our guest at our own whimsy
as something that we could not understand
the meaning of, and therefore had to own.

4

And when I saw the horse for real it appeared
as a *copy* of that horse on that pure field
on that eternal day when it had seemed
I could have stepped into the very sky—
or that I *had* stepped into the sky.
When they were raping me in the useless temple
there was a moment when the shame and pain
were so great that I seemed to burst out of myself
and float again up there, bodiless,
peering down with only curiosity
at this helpless girl pinned bleeding on the tiles—
Yes, whirled by pain and terror—that I looked on
just like the gods whose consciences we killed
to keep our own were once said to have done.
It's the present we're forbidden to believe.

The Phoenix

Being ash, being dust,
being what's left on the plate,
being the bungalow with a moss-eaten roof
a stone's throw off from the new glass house,

being bone and gristle,
being biomass,
being something stuck to the fridge floor
whiffing of a long-turned tide,
being shredded, unsought secrets,
being car exhaust,
being half-buried rusted-out bedsprings
sleeping it off in the woods,

being what was washed from the photo by the years,
being what will never wash,
being what's in the storm drain hurrying off,

the dust flaring up in the comet's tail,
the toenail clippings feeling around under the rug,
the sticks laid out on the highway after a storm,
the pennies on the dashboard short of a dollar,
the hollow core of an old swamp cedar,
the crumpled butt of the sweetest cigarette

you ever had, I am
everywhere, and I demand my wings.

The Idealist

Friends, I am sick of the world, sick
of the way it holds its hand out and
yanks it back. You will say
I am feeling sorry for myself and I
am sick of that, too. I am sick of every day's
demand to be loved, it's ever-fresh
sunrises and moonrises and
rains and winds and heartbreakingly quiet
snows coming down like the hush
of young mothers. You will say
I am bitter. I know. You will say
I should get a life—and I have
tried! Do you think it's for nothing
I spent ten years belting songs from barstools,
hitting on my coworkers, slogging through
the first fifty pages of a motherload
of "notable books"? My level of commitment
should not be in question here. If I say
the night is as boring as a long flight,
it's because I have been up in it
for years. You will say
I am trying to pick a fight. Oh, friends,
nothing could be less true. It isn't you
I blame for this stalled train of day
after day after day with the same
smirk on its face, ringing you out of sleep
like a telemarketer. Though even my dreams
are getting old—the same old lovers
traipsing around the same old hallways,
the same old feeling that something
has been irredeemably lost.
If there's one thing I'm sick of,
it's that. You will say, I'm being

melodramatic—as though
I were the problem! Friends,
if it were up to me, there'd be
a moratorium on boredom,
and dancing wouldn't be so ridiculous,
or *Ulysses* so inscrutable,
or instruments so hard to play,
and if you wanted to feel a certain way
that's how you'd feel, end of story.

Jansson

*Chief Ranger Robert Jansson recalling the Mann Gulch Fire of 1949, which took place in his district.**

We descended into the gulch from the same ridge†
where Rumsey and Sallee had crossed to safety, finding
the crevice in the twelve-foot-high rim rocks
that ran like a defensive wall along it
not eight hours after the blowup, ground soft ash
still warm in places, stalagmite spikes of trees
charred back to rock, some lashing out
occasional tongues of flame from their hollow cores
so that the whole slope flickered in the darkness,
here and there popping out with exploding resin

and now and then the ground trembled slightly
to acknowledge that another spike had fallen
somewhere, in silence, in the dark. We heard
a human cry below us and the smell
of burning human flesh rose with it, thick
as blood, a smell you feel in your chest and arms,
a smell that brands itself somewhere inside you.

"Please don't come around and look at my face," then "Say,
it didn't take you fellows long to get here."
It was Sylvia, who somehow stood on a sloping rock,
charred beyond recognition except as silhouette,
who somehow was talking as though he still belonged
to the living who had jumped from that airplane
twelve hours ago and joked about where they'd sleep.

His hands were burned to charred clubs, and I peeled
an orange and fed it to him, section by section.
He was cold and some of the rescue party stripped
their shirts and wrapped him up. And for a while
it seemed his needs were not so different
from those of the living. He made a big fuss

about his boots, and we found them, and he was glad.
The doctor told me he'd be dead by ten.

The others had already made it there. We found
their bodies, one at a time, going down the hill
with Sylvia, still talking, in the litter:
Harrison fallen forward on his knees,
Raba just a charred stump of a man.
There was nothing left but trinkets: flashlights, food tins,
a Catholic cross scorched into Hellman's chest.
Some things were flung a hundred feet uphill
by the blast that blew their clothes away like vapors.

The general appearance was that a terrific draft
of superheated air of tremendous velocity
had swept up the hill, exploding all
inflammable material, causing a wall
of flame six hundred feet high to roll over the ridge,
is how I described, in my report, the landscape
that appeared when daylight came. I might have said something
of the feeling that some thin veneer on life
had been curled back, that a façade had crumbled
and revealed the inner ashes of the world—
that on that slope, the fantasy of life
had woken from its dream—but to what end?

I don't sleep much any more. I smell that night
whenever I close my eyes, a putrid draft
climbing upslope toward me from Mann Gulch.
It may be green again there now. It must be.
It may be that it's possible to forget things.
Those questions ring to me like so much jargon.
What I stay up thinking about is wind direction—

how it shifts near gorges at certain times of the day.
How fuel types react to changes in RH.

How many seconds, exactly, Harrison
could have kept running with the air sacs charred in his lungs—
and where, again, it was that Sylvia left
his boots, the boots he knew he'd have to have
for the long walk out, down the black slope
to the cool river.

*The facts and the quotations are from Norman MacLean's *Young Men and Fire*.

Song of the Detainee

I may have done something. Who could say?
I only know this number now,
this cell, this shit-stained floor, this day
that like a prayer repeats and repeats itself.

Sleep and pain, no meaning now.
They mean as little as the words that come
when they pull my head from the water
and let the bloody snot run from my lungs.

The only evidence that I'm not dead
is my heart and bowels continuing their spasms
like outposts of an extremist faction
whose true beliefs I have never understood.

The questions never change.
They speak themselves, and answer back.
My name is Abdurahman Khadr.
My crime is weakness. In all of history

is there any other? Who could say?
I only know this number now,
this day, this prompted speech I give them
in a language I once called my own,

promising to give them back their freedom.

When I Found Out I Was Dying

When I found out I was dying I went to visit
each of my friends from over the years,
so many of whom I had long forgotten
the connection with that had made us

so happy then in the high altitude silence
of 3 A.M. with the city and all its
garbage washed down to bone or there

in the snow-lit morning of the deep woods or where
the tin-can clash of a bar had found
its voice and its forgotten song—truces

we walked into with our weapons drawn
and left cross-hatching plans for new towns—

and we sat long hours talking about the times
that mattered, no longer ashamed
of all the times that didn't, which we found
had ceased to be, like unremembered dreams,

and I saw that what I had often thought of as
a thin and unimportant life had really been
the journey of a god's time on earth

and when we said goodbye there were none of the usual
lies about retracing some old road trip
or looking up some third who had only been
a witness, or of that island in the Keys where each
would write that definitive novel—no, there was no

future to escape to this time—from each other,
from the gravity of what we had done—

and I was happy in a way I had never known

though also, of course, sad,
that I, too, had to die to save the world.

Varykino

It's that only after Zhivago and Lara
had crossed near half the country
and exiled themselves to a town made ghost
by the revolution, both of them hunted
for the silliest and most real reasons
(family heritage, speaking one's mind)
and had moved into one of the empty houses,

it's that only then could they begin
to live, on something like page four hundred,
just as they'd lost all hope of living
in the other sense: the sense of having
food and wood to survive a Russian winter,
the sense of believing the one you love will be
stoking a fire and bustling with linen
a week from now, or in the spring, saying,
The point is that the gift of love
is like any other gift—it's this

that haunts me about *Doctor Zhivago*...
and Lear, who never loved until
an hour before they killed his daughter,
and the bursts in Beethoven's late quartets,
the home key battering down the door
at last and falling face-down. The joy
I've known seems always blooming

at the ends of things, an afterthought,
or a truth that can only finally be said
over a shoulder, leaving—snuggling
with Kate the other night, months after
we'd agreed to let it go so many
times our lines were worn

translucent, playfully switching
TV channels on each other
during bathroom trips, her gently
masturbating me when I got horny
in a place that felt like an abandoned town—
everything there but sustenance. I don't know

what to do with that. Lara
was trundled off to Siberia and Zhivago
stumbled on with failing heart to die
a few years later, puking
on a station platform but that last night
in Varykino he stayed up
all night writing poems in that
town of a thousand houses empty
as a cello, whispering over and over,
Lord! Lord! And all this for me?

Kicking Russell Out of the Band

When he got there, a ring of us
were leaned on cars outside Terry's garage—
guys around forty and me, twenty-seven—
when he got there in that little pickup
frail with rust, an aquarium of tools
through the truck cap window. It was
Terry who told him—for once in weeks
no anger in his voice about
the lagging tempo, or, *That's not calypso!*
And then there was a silence not unlike
the half-a-sec at the end of a tune, mouthpiece
at my lips, not yet
the clatter of life again, and Russell
went blank as a lottery winner—

Russell, who banged at two-by-fours all day
so he could play drums at night, who had been
with them since the first
cow-pasture-fests at Jason's farm,
me always finding out after,
their names in a myth
of sunshine and hippy girls. "Chris,
did you go along with this?" he asked,
which, I remember, surprised me—
I was still on the theory of people just
driving away. And when I saw him

at the bank last week, thirteen years later,
and asked him, "Are you playing any music?"
there was a moment in which
we were still standing there at Terry's garage,
me leaning back on a car like a shy boy playing
cool at a dance, saying, "Yah, I did,"
believing this was a decision

about lagging tempos, thinking
it was actually an option to side with beauty.
And then Russell looked at me and said, “All the time.”
And then I just drove away.

John and Jackie Kennedy on a Boat Deck, 1960

Does it matter that they were so beautiful
and adored—by way, at least,
of their images? It's the old
grade-school question, I know, but it's
difficult to look on such perfect hair—
at sea, no less—and not drift back
to Jodi Carmichael with her laughing doll face
whom I, too, wrote a yes/no note
in fifth grade, who turned up
outside a bar recently looking
ordinary, and maybe still a little stunned.
As a bald man with certain
antisocial characteristics—
as an American, damn it—I want to know:
does it matter that John and Jackie Kennedy
were so beautiful and adored? Because
they look as though they're king and queen
in those gorgeous, above-it-all faces, the placid
yacht-peppered harbor where no one punches
a clock or chews with an open mouth
behind them like a dream. And me on the wall
at twenty-six, grinning and strong,
still holding the rope I came down on, one spot
of blue on the cliff above me like
a long-awaited breath—was it
only a dream? Does it
mean anything? Let's
put it to a vote, shall we?
Yes or no, that's all I'm asking.

Providence

That painting is a map
with people living on it.

That symphony is a set of instructions
with geraniums growing from the clefts.

That architecture is a luke-warm ribcage
woven together with tiny songs.

That poem is an argument
fluttering in the midst of a migration.

That belief is a roof
with starlight shining through its perforations.

People in History

They couldn't know the shame of their condition.
Their ridiculous dress. Their conspicuous lack
of plumbing and public transportation.
Their hopelessly benighted views
on diseases and the solar system.

The pride with which they gaze from paintings
is the pride of children in a pageant
who have just given birth to a doll.
They seem to think they have conquered the very thing
we now understand will ruin them completely.

They believed in gods that turned out to be broken statues.
They built walls that may as well have been picket fences.
They gave speeches we mainly remember now
for their apparently sincere dead metaphors.
And they are, of course, utterly hopeless:

their final dates now seal like royal wax
their last, deluded missives.
The only consolation that we have
is that they never saw it coming,
that they believed until the end

that rather than having found new continents
with all the genocides and revolutions
and trails of tears and endless breaking ground
that would have to follow such a thing,
they had merely found a back door to an old one.

This Dreaming of You Again

I'm beginning to suspect it puts me
right up there with Ptolemy, this
dreaming of you, his stars,
in spite of the facts, forever circling
the regal earth—and all the popes
who loved him. Of course, it may be

that you have become a symbol—
my subconscious, or God, or *whatever*
throwing your face onto my screen
when I need to remember what it was
to trust in the worth of anything
that strongly. Is that

a symbol? Because if you were standing
for something else, it was
also burning inside you. "Three times

have I seen the Great Buck," the Inuit tells
the young hero in a movie I am
probably paraphrasing badly, "Once
in the flush of first manhood, once
at the height of my powers, and last night,
when I knew that I would die." Is all this just

the bright spots blanking out the actual thing
after looking at you directly? If I have

a tribe to save, I don't know where we live
or how we shape our arrowheads.
I no longer seem to know what life
is supposed to be *like*, M. Maybe

that's the reason for your face last night,
you pulling back the covers and beaming—
yes, beaming—at me. The *reason?* "How in the world

shall I act?" White Eagle said to the general
who was showing him his new home
of rocks and dust. Ptolemy demonstrated

with excruciating calculation how
it was all possible. Have I not yet, M,
at forty now, figured out a way
to see what's really there? Ten years after,

can it still be you? Is that
love, or creationism? I can't explain, either,

why all these Native Americans
are in this poem. It's almost as though
they were already here when I started.

Tom's House

Tom's living room, which was long, where we cranked
Aerosmith through chest-high speakers
until the piano hummed at the other end.

Tom's barn where his father the orthodontist
kept horses and a tremendous loft of hay.

Tom's bedroom where we crashed
after lurching the car in late from drinking
where he still had a bunk bed because his parents
were cool with his friends staying over
and I would stare at the ceiling just over my face
as we talked about girls and all the gearings
of our secret life in which there was stolen liquor
and cigarettes and slick, quick touches
of panties and always the next thing past
a fast bend on a dark road, Tom pretending
he couldn't make the corner,
both of us screeching with laughter.

Tom's kitchen with its oversize appliances
and miles of counter where once, at least,
we had the place full of kids from his high school,
drinking and scheming on each other's new bodies,
buoyed for hours by the light-footed rage inside us—
where his parents had a whole drawer just for stale bread
and where one time we ate most of an entire ham
in the middle of the night, pulling
the slippery, cold pieces off with our fingers.

Tom's upstairs bathroom, painfully white,
waking up drunk to suck tap water from my hands.

And last night, in a dream, Tom's
ice-cream shop—his parents had bought one,
and we sat with them and ate enormous sundaes,
layers of ice cream and whipped cream and sauces—

and nothing important had changed: his parents
were politely and inscrutably supplying the ice cream
and we were devouring it as though
we still hadn't gotten enough of being sixteen
where you never feel full or not horny
or like you're a guest in someone else's house.

The Romantic Version

It's the middle of the night, almost smack.
I've slept a little, and woken up, and eaten some cheese.
I dozed off at six, reading yet another Kundera.
You can do this when you live alone.
You can set up a chair between the house and the driveway
and smoke a cigarette under the stars.
I suppose that's the romantic version.
The others, well.
The woodstove is snapping in the kitchen
in the dark I've left there to come to the study.
The black is at the windows.
It isn't that I don't like people, not anymore.
As Bukowski had it, and I mean this
in the kindest way possible, I just feel better
when they're not around.
That's also, I suppose, the romantic version.
At forty, one begins to think about why
he is the way he is.
One begins to consider if he's just an asshole.
Clearly something else is needed.
Today out on the job site we were singing
"Kissed by the Rose of a Grave"
for the pure lugubrious fun of it,
digging holes and moving rocks,
and I got them laughing with a particularly syrupy
rendering of Seal's falsetto
and found that I had to hold back
from ripping through the whole tortured thing.
"It's a useless ability," I muttered once about singing
to some successful, withering writers in New Jersey
and to my surprise, they took issue with that.
We were listening to karaoke at the time.
Though I still hold out the hope that all our losses

will ultimately prove to be forms of entertainment.
I suppose that makes me a believer, of sorts.
I suppose you want something, my mother loves
to quote a waitress from a long-closed diner
as saying to her once in the '70s.
It is 2009.
I will read on Saturday for a thing to promote
the need to reduce emissions.
I'll follow the usual train of SUVs
to read to the usual crowd of the slightly loony.
Safety begins with me, it chirps
on the protective glasses we wear at work.
God, I hate America.
Kundera was talking about nostalgia,
the yearning for some lost and golden land.
It's not like we have that many topics really.
It's funny, though, how sometimes
I'll see a picture of a place I drive by every morning
and it looks like the world I've been trying to get to
my whole life. I do miss Ellie.
I sometimes even miss Miranda.
I'm a human being, damn it,
as someone cracked on the job today
when the two-way radio answered a broken transmission,
Unit calling, this is dispatch.
A lake, maybe, with the low boughs hanging into it
or a road taking one slow bend
into a cloud of branches thick with green.
It isn't that I don't like my life—
though I think I'll like it better when it's not around.
It *would* be nice to be loved again.

It would be nice to win the Pulitzer
and have withering writers nod their solemn assent
at *Singing is a useless ability.*
Can you win the Pulitzer for saying
I suppose you want something?

IV

Reasons to Be Happy

Because of the ice sheets
Because in a dream
Because of the inch-deep layers that used to be cities
Because of what Marlowe said
I mean what happened to him
I mean why it happened

Because we already have Beethoven and Berryman
Because of what happened to them
I mean what O'Hara said
That dark and purifying wave

Because we can't help it anyway
Because sadness is so cluttered
Because you can't do better
You

Because even though we know life is only using us
I mean how rotten we feel *afterwards*
Because of China syndrome
Because you have two choices
Maybe only one
I could have said *after words*—
Because no one ever is
Because those that are you wish weren't
Because of the side effects of the cure for death

Because of the pharmacist in a tight shirt
Because it's so hard to continually keep from knowing
Because from here the whole place is a toy
Because exhaustion is a form of knowledge
Because you cannot say anything
Without unsaying something else

I mean how once you touch the match to the wood
I might as well be talking to the Trojans
What is UP dude
Because deep in the wooden horse of sadness
Because I could just go on and on like this
Because we've let in just about everything else

Sonnets to Elise

1.

There's a paltriness now to things. The metaphor
of having stared at the sun seems right. And there's
that farawayness of after a loud concert
in the fish tank of the self, pulse in the ears
like the flapping of film when the screen goes white—
will anyone even remember the flapping of film? One thing
cuts in to replace another. Before that first night
I was pleased with the taste of coffee, the cool mourning
of cars in the tree-filled distance, my job, my poems,
and now that all feels more like—what? Not nothing. But
as though each thing were only the thing it is,
not singing of some greater world with what
the gods have given it, gone now as they are:
a voice, a heart, and light—light everywhere.

2.

In Beirut bombs are suffering the little children,
in Baghdad's morgues the cordwood bodies wait
in the earrings and fillings by which ye shall know them
and it's easier for a shotgun of the Janjaweed
to enter a vagina than the façade
of democracy to open up one cunt hair—and I'm
more likely to get censored for saying that
than all the droners of the Pentagon. This time
I fear there is no reconciliation:
that *cannot* be this world in which we love,
where, while field crickets cut loose, Jessye Norman
frees Schubert's *Lieder* cell by cell, and move
by move bliss mates its yearning. Oh, Elise.
I must seat them both, but have no hope for peace.

3.

Ellie, you've just gone home and I'm left here
with only this huge paradise that spans
the crisp-misted fields, the sky from ear to ear
with something we've named *August* for lack of hands
to glide along the hips of such things. Awe
is the only appropriate emotion for what
we last night standing in the field's mind saw,
some dirty window busted, the sky's glass perfect.
As though everything you thought were true were true,
I said out loud, but you were with me then,
and words came easy, each one seeming new
to its fresh thought, like when we were in the basement
of a friend's house that first night we talked, gone down
to begin this love—thinking, to look around.

What For

What for, then, this bay
of roiling, these mountains standing
stock in their hunched files,
these four geese fast-forwarded by
like a movie kiss by the wind in its
hysterical vibrato—branches,
ferns, swamp grass and tiny bush stems
all quivering like mad
in their little cliques, none
taking one step out its
appointed place—what for, since not

human happiness. And this

light that is making metal
of the rain-soaked picnic table, slate
of the walls of waves and draping
bridal gauze above the rounded
shoulders of the most left-behind hills—
how else to see such
blatant references, like a
hostage answering the door whose eyes

keep darting meaningfully to the side
while she says, "Yes,
it's a nice day, isn't it?"

Beth

At some house your parents rented,
on some afternoon after school,
and with some friend of mine who occupies
a friend-like shape killing time with cassettes,
we made out furiously on a couch,
you coming full-breasted into me
after two or three cups of whatever we were drinking
had made my wrong clothes and wrong friends
negligible, you all soft business
and bulky sweater, the sheer impossibility of it
suspended by booze, you coming into me,
eyes closed against the intimacy,
again and again for hours
in just the same way—no progress
of my hand from breast to inner thigh,
no dangling ends of a conversation
we kept snagging back up like Tarzan's ropes
to swing us across the jungle of high school romance:
just that one motion, and only that one night.
I think of it still, though, often.
Whatever exit I took I don't remember,
only that the next day at school
you waited outside the instrument room
to rapidly say there was nothing
between us and I think I took it
fairly well for a band geek in the wrong style corduroys;
if I said anything back, it wasn't
the kind of thing you regret forever.
It wasn't until that summer,
the last time I ever saw you—
when you came back from a beach
to my friend's motel room
and drank with us, and slipped your hand
into my hand when we left the room

in such a way that it felt like we'd been
doing that for years, walking
towards beach screams at the end of the street
because you had promised to meet someone,
because there must always be a point
beyond which there can be no more—
that I saw that had I pushed it
I could have had what I wanted:
to have spent so many more afternoons
at your house, drinking whatever you had
with whoever else was there and making out
furiously for hours, eyes closed, groping
at the same place over and over.

The Stepping Stones

Leaning up against the cut-up pieces
of an old footbridge at lunch, we are
talking about politics: the Copenhagen
global-warming summit, Afghanistan,
an interview with Nader who said
that only the super-rich
can save us now. The little beach
looks out on a pond between two mountains
that cup the clouds between them
in a light-washed blue. The ozone days
are over, and it's like the dust has blown
from the trees that porcupine the ledges.
Cars drift somewhere in that distant groan
as constant here as breathing. "Too little
too late," I answer Clark about the talks.
"We're basically screwed," adds Michael, and laughs
a laugh that seems to slump down
with his shoulders, a little lower
since the birth of his third. Clark,
in his fifties now, in his tie-dyed bandana,
says the youth is really getting
involved, you know? "There's so much positive
energy out there right now," he says
through puffs of an American Spirit. Behind us,
giant stepping stones span the outlet.
They were built by George Dorr in 1915,
who gave all the land we can see from here
and died penniless. In the picture we're using
to set each stone as it was, he looks
like a normal man: distracted, tired,
trapped in the era's costume. "The youth
is sexting and listening to Fox News," Dave says,
and recloses his eyes, up late last night
with his girlfriend out of town. The leaves

have started turning, single trees
gone suddenly red in a valley of green
like clear, high trumpet notes and the season
of RVs has started, tin garages
leaned out on shoulders all along
the Loop Road, stern retirees snapping
photos from their tailpipes. Last night
I dreamt I had traveled back to college
and stood looking up at the house where I had
drunk away two entire years. "Sexting?"
says Clark, snuffing out his butt with his
thick, former-boxer's hands. He has declared
he's going to quit so many times
we've started a pool on the boss's whiteboard
where everyone's guess is a joke:
This Sunday—okay, some Sunday;
Right after the funeral;
When the poles reverse, and now that it's been weeks:
When Gary finally erases the whiteboard.
"I just see all this positive energy," he continues,
lighting another American Spirit.
"That's got nothing to do with it, Clark," Michael says
and we all laugh, even Clark, because
the beauty is all that ever feels real, and Dave,
without opening his eyes, mumbles,
"And I think your stone's crooked."

Christian Barter's first book, *The Singers I Prefer*, was a finalist for the Lenore Marshall Prize. His poetry has appeared in *Ploughshares*, *The Georgia Review*, *The American Scholar*, and elsewhere, and it has been featured on *Poetry Daily*, *Verse Daily* and Garrison Keillor's *The Writer's Almanac*. He has received residency fellowships from Yaddo and the MacDowell Colony and a Hodder Fellowship in Creative Writing at Princeton University. He is an editor at the *Beloit Poetry Journal* and supervises a trail crew in Bar Harbor, Maine.